PETROLEUM COLLECTIBLES

Rick Pease

77 Lower Valley Road, Atglen, PA 19310

Dedication

This book is dedicated to everyone who has bought, sold, or collected pieces of our past.

Designed by Ian Robertson

Printed in China
ISBN: 0-7643-0202-7

Published by Schiffer Publishing, Ltd.
77 Lower Valley Road
Atglen, PA 19310
Phone: (610) 593-1777
Fax: (610) 593-2002

Please write for a free catalog.
This book may be purchased from the publisher.
Please include $2.95 for shipping.
Try your bookstore first.

We are interested in hearing from
authors with book ideas on related subjects.

Table of Contents

Acknowledgments

Many thanks to the special friends who contributed to this book:

Bill Brown, Tim Dye, David Anderson, Terry St. Clair, Nick Ciovica, Fred Hartson, Mark Cioni, Dwaine Buck, Tom Davidson, Randy Sachs, Aubrey Burke, Kyle Moore, Howard Clayburn, Charles Middleton, Kim and Mary Kokles, Scott Benjamin, Mike Worley, Barry Baker, Norm Rubenstein, Mike O'Hern, Charles Shaver, Wayne Story, Vick and Sara Raupe, Leo Mathieu, Kenny Boone, Richard Amistadi.

Introduction

As we reminisce about the good ol' days, we can visualize all the roadside relics that made a trip in the car interesting and pleasurable.

The gasoline landscape along the highway provided us with colorful, artful logos of the gasoline companies. There was the Standard logo, which was one of the earliest, if not the earliest. We also appreciated the beauty of other logos such as the Texaco Star, the Magnolia Flower, the Flying Red Horse...to name just a few.

The statuesque silhouettes of the old pumps provided us with a variety of shapes, sizes, and colors—unlike today's computerized gasoline pumps. Through the artistic pictorial design, some of the old cans containing gasoline and oil products actually told a story about the company and its product.

Stopping at one of the old service stations was a treat. Most of the gasoline and oil companies had colorful and useful give-aways. These give-aways have retained their sentimental value even today while their monetary value has increased.

In this book I hope to take you on a trip down the highways of yesteryear. I have included a wide array of pumps, globes, signs (American and foreign), oil cans, maps, license plate attachments, and salt and pepper shakers.

I hope you enjoy the scenery of the past.

Salt & Pepper Sets

This section of the book is from Mark Cioni's collection. Mark provided the pictures and prices.

These collectibles are referred to correctly as, "Plastic Figural Gas Pump Salt and Pepper Sets." They were molded in Missouri during the late 1940s through the early 1970s and were service station give-aways. An individual owner could order no less than fifty sets. Corporate headquarters sent out official colors to their company-owned stations. The Phillips 'Orange' color, for example, is common. But independent owners could order fifty of their own color. Phillips on white, for example, is not common for this very reason.

It is unlikely that these sets will be reproduced successfully as there are five different body styles, seventeen meter styles, eight different sight glass styles, and far too many different colors. Each has been documented and researched.

There are now 120+ different sets known to exist.

A complete documented guide to these give-away sets is for sale for, $15 ppd. It's called "The Official Gas Pump Salt and Pepper Guide" by Mark Cioni. The guide is 31 pages and includes photos (black & white) of most all the sets. The address to write to is: Mark Cioni, 707 Oakwood Road, East Peoria, IL, 61611.

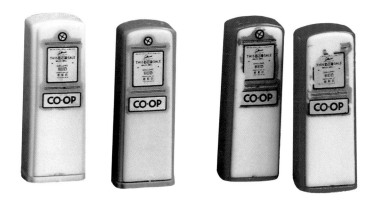

(left) CO-OP, green and yellow from Canada, $30-40
(right) CO-OP, red and white from the USA, $25-35

(left) Conoco, white with green base, $25-35
(right) Skelly, red, $60-75

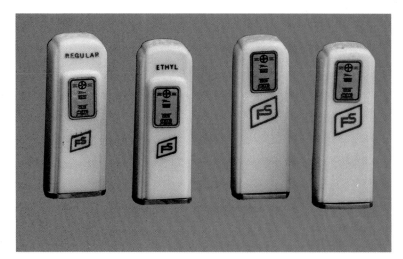

(left) Farm Service, white with blue base, Regular and Ethyl, $65-75
(right) Farm Service, white with blue base, Tall doors, $55-75

(left) Sinclair, white with red trim and base, Rd 119, $50-65
(right) Sinclair, white with red trim and base, Power X, $55-65

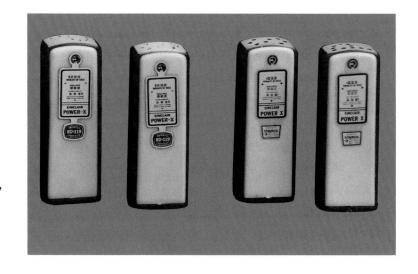

(left) Atlantic, red with blue base—Regular, red and white with blue base—Premium, $50-60
(right) Standard, blue and white—Super Premium, red and white—Regular, $70-85

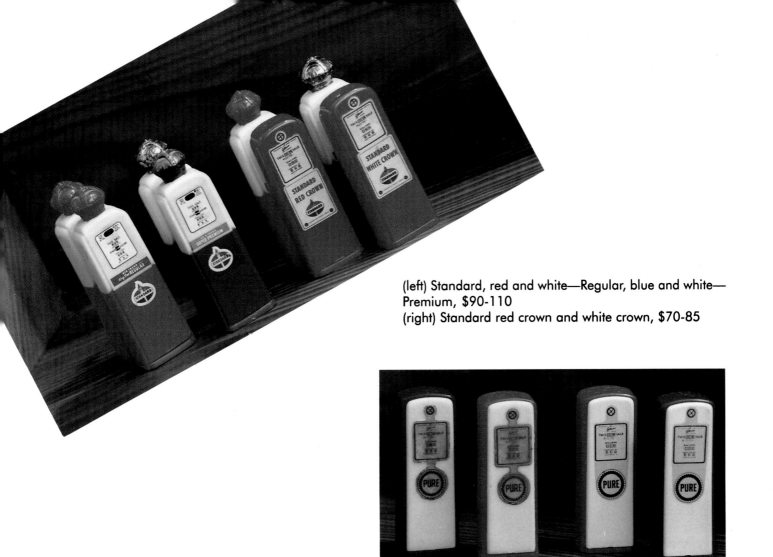

(left) Standard, red and white—Regular, blue and white—
Premium, $90-110
(right) Standard red crown and white crown, $70-85

Pure (two sets), notice the difference in decals, $75-80

(left) Universal, yellow with blue trim, $60-70 pair
(right) El Paso, red and white—Premium, blue and white—
Regular, No Price Available

Mobilgas, red
Mobilgas Special, red and white,
$50-65

(left) DX, ethyl, $60-70
(right) DX, Boron, $60-75

(left) Deep Rock, yellow and red—Premium, yellow and blue—Regular, $80-95
(right) DX, white with red base, white with red base, Boron, $50-65

(left) Richfield, yellow with blue base—Hydrogen Powered, yellow with blue base—High Octane, $60-75
(right) Richfield, yellow with blue base, Ethyl yellow with blue base—High Octane, $65-75

(left) City Service, red—Super 5-D, green—Milemaster, $45-55
(right) City Service, green and white, red and white—5-D Premium, $50-60

Salt and Pepper with miniature tire rack (generic), No Price Available

(left) Phillips 66, square top—Regular, $15-25
(right) Phillips 66, round top—Flite Fuel, $30-40

(left) Phillips 66, flat top—Regular and Ethyl, $15-25
(right) Phillips 66, flat top—Regular and Flite Fuel, $20-30

Four pairs of Shell
gasoline pumps:
(from left to right)
$70-80, $60-75,
$70-85, $75-85

(left) Philgas canisters, $65-75
(right) Phillips 66, blue and red, $50-60 pair

(left) Esso extra—red, white, and blue, $10-15
(right) Esso extra and Humble—red, $20-30

(left) Amoco, green and yellow, $80-95
(right) Barney's, white with green base, No Price Available

(left) Hancock, yellow and white—Super Powered, red and white—Regular, $140-150
(right) Marathon, white with blue base, $70-85

(left) Texaco, red Fire Chief, silver Sky Chief, $25-35
(right) Texaco, red Fire Chief, silver Sky Chief with Petrox, $85-95

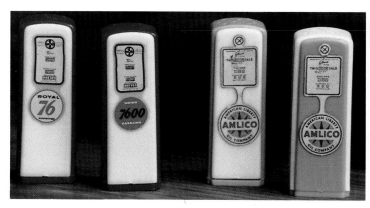

(left) Union 76, blue and white—Royal, blue and white—7600, $80-90
(right) Amlico, pale blue and white, $80-95

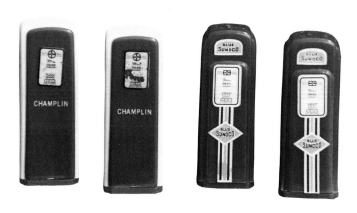

(left) Champlin, blue and white with red base, $60-70
(right) Sunoco, blue with yellow trim, $80-95

(left) Farm Bureau CO-OP, white with red/black trim, $50-60
(right) Mobil Farm Set, $25-35

Mobiloil Special, silver miniature cans (with carrying case), $45-55

(left to right, prices quoted are per pair): Zenith, red and white, $40-50
Cities Service, red, white, and blue, $50-60
Shell, white with red base, $60-70

(left) Philgas canisters, $10-15
(right) Hausgas canisters, $10-15

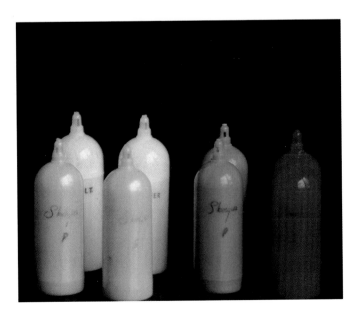

Skelgas, four pair, $10-15

Fina, $90-110

Maps

Gulf-Florida, $18-22

Royal—Iowa, $13-15

Marathon—Texas, $20-25

Marathon—Indiana, $26-30

Conoco—Illinois, $26-30

(reverse side of map)

Conoco—Arizona, 1930, $26-30

(reverse side of map)

Richfield—California, $20-25

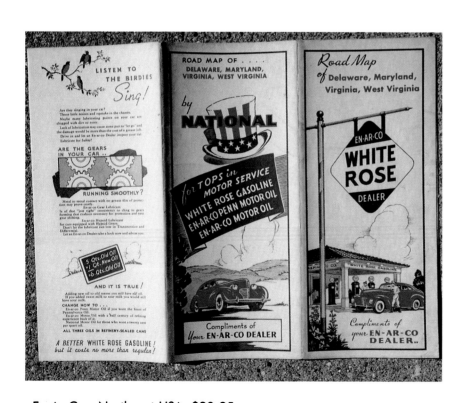

En-Ar-Co—Northeast USA, $20-25

Hudson Oil Co.—Central USA, $12-15

14

Standard Oil—Mississippi, $35-48

Phillips 66—Missouri, $25-35

Standard Oil—Florida, $35-48

Standard Oil—Georgia, $40-51

Phillips 66—Missouri (1933), $25-35

Phillips 66—Missouri, $20-30

Phillips 66—Iowa, 1935, $20-30

Pan-Am Mexican Petroleum Corp.—New York, $25-33

Coryell 70-Iowa, $28-36

Derby Oil Co.—Missouri, $22-32

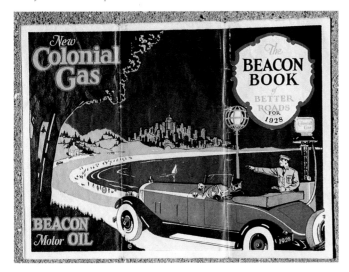

Colonial Gas—Beacon Book of Better Roads, $28-38

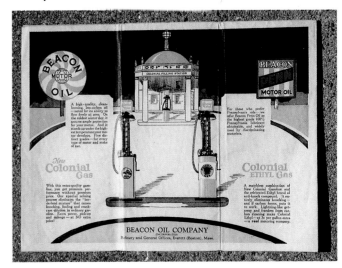

Colonial Gas, Beacon Oil, $28-38

Panhandle Refining Co.—Texas, $18-25

Pathfinder Petroleum—Western States, $18-25

Deep Rock Oil Corp.—Illinois, $25-35

Deep Rock Oil Corp.—Illinois (1932), $28-38

Deep Rock Oil Corp.—Minnesota, $18-28

Deep Rock Oil Corp.—Indiana, $18-28

Shell—New England and New York,
$11-16

Kendall Refining Co.—Pennsylvania,
Ohio, $17-23

Champlin—Missouri, $12-17

Globe Products—Oklahoma, $17-23

Esso Standard Oil Co.—Middle Atlantic States, $17-23

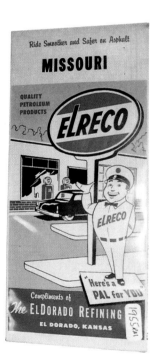

Eldorado Refining—Missouri (1955), $8-11

Pure Oil—North and South Carolina, $11-16

Frontier Refining—Arizona and New Mexico (1957), $11-16

Frontier Refining—Idaho, Montana, Wyoming, $11-16

Skelly Oil—Kansas, $17-23

White Eagle Refining—Kansas (1928), $48-58

Alaskan Petroleum
Corp.—Alaska,
$6-11

Imperial Refineries—
Minnesota (1950),
$7-11

Bay—Florida (1960),
$10-13

Husky Hi-Power—
Montana & Idaho,
$10-13

Wilcox—Kansas, $11-16

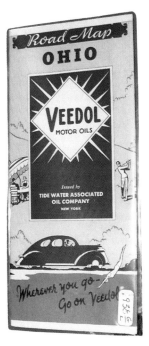

American Oil Co.—North and South Carolina, $28-38

Veedol—Ohio (1938), $10-13

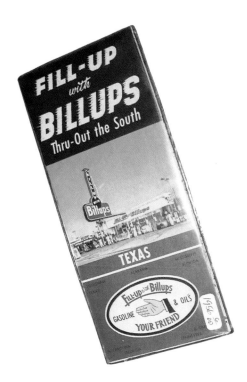

Billups—Texas (1956), $11-16   Falcon—Kansas (1955), $8-11   Martin—Illinois (1957), $11-16

23

Signal Gas—Washington and Oregon, $17-23

(reverse side of Signal Gas)

Sun Oil Co.—Florida, $25-35

Sun Oil Co.—Florida, $17-23

Sun Oil Co.—Ohio, Indiana, Kentucky, $17-23

Kendall Refining Co.—New York and
New England, $12-17

Mobilgas—Western States, $12-18

Standard Oil Co.—New Jersey (1931), $22-30

Marathon (World War II)—Michigan, $30-35

United Motor Courts—New Orleans, $12-18

Illinois Farm Supply—Illinois, $21-26

Humble—Texas, $17-21

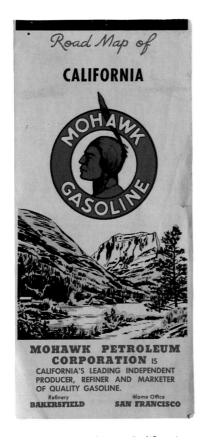

Mohawk Gasoline—California,
$17-21

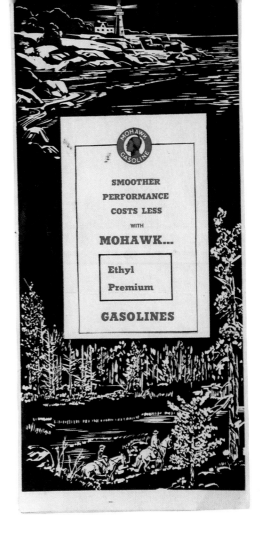

(reverse side of Mohawk Gasoline)

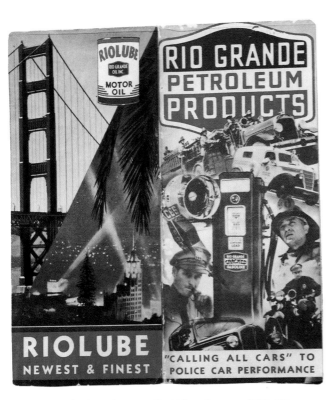

Rio Grande Petroleum—So West States, $38-52

Associated Oil
Co.—Oregon,
Idaho—Mon-
tana, $12-16

Associated Oil Co.—California and Nevada, $12-16

Associated Oil Co.—California, $20-25

Sinclair—Missouri (1932), $48-56

Standard Oil Co. (Sohio)—Ohio (1935), $12-16

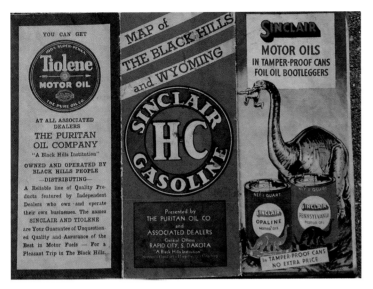

Sinclair—Black Hills and Wyoming, $54-61

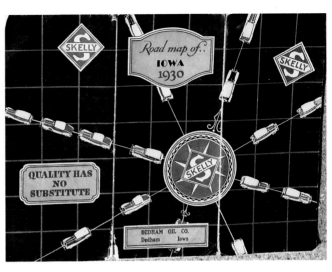

Skelly—Iowa (1930), $19-26

D-X—Iowa, $27-32

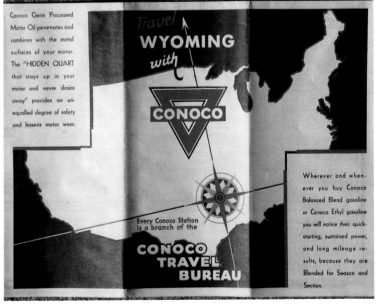

Conoco—Wyoming, $17-21

Associated Oil Co.—New Jersey,
$8-11

Associated Oil Co.—New Hampshire
and Vermont, $8-11

Sovereign Service—Colorado, $12-16

Standard Oil Co.—Wisconsin (1934), $17-21

Gulf Refining—Florida, $17-21

Gulf Refining—Kentucky and Tennessee, $12-16

Derby Oil Co.—Mississippi to Rockies (1925), $38-51

Richfield—California, $20-26

Richfield—San Francisco Bay Area, $12-16

Richfield—California, $25-32

Richfield—New Jersey, $20-27

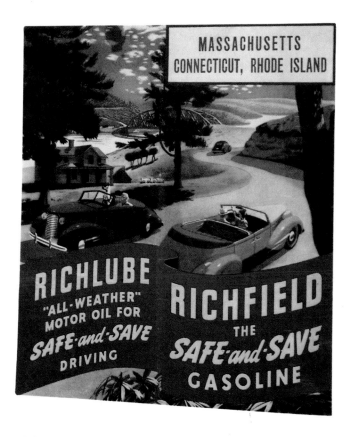

Richfield—Massachusetts, Connecticut, Rhode Island, $25-31

Universal Motor Oils—Kansas, $25-31

Cushing Refining—Missouri, $20-26

Pure Oil Co.—So. Eastern States, $20-26

Pure Oil Co., $20-26

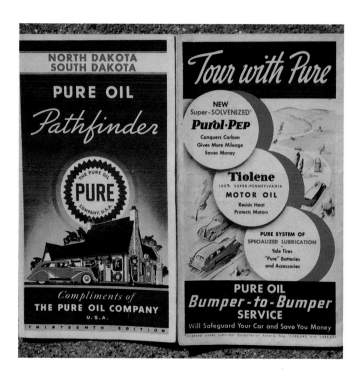

Pure Oil Co.—North and South Dakota, $21-28

Johnson Oil Products—Oklahoma, $20-26

Frontier—California, $12-16

Cosden—Colorado, Nevada, Utah, $12-16

Associated Oil Co.—Indiana (1940), $25-31

Tydol—New York, $20-26

Mobilgas—Oregon, Washington, $12-16

Associated Oil Co.—New Hampshire,
Vermont, $12-16

White Eagle—Missouri, Iowa, Illinois (1932), $35-42

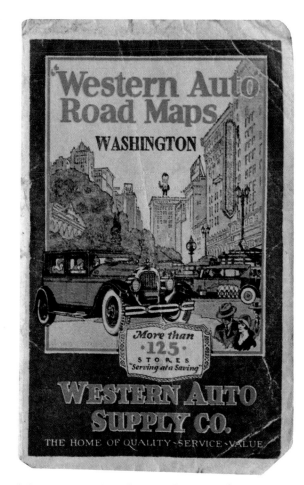

Western Auto Supply—Washington, $8-11

Signal Products—California, No Price Available

Signal Products—Washington, Oregon, Idaho, Montana, $20-26

Phillips 66—Kansas, $17-21

(reverse side of Phillips 66)

Phillips 66—Kansas, $20-26

Derby Oil—Colorado, $12-16

Simpson Oil Co.—Missouri, $17-21

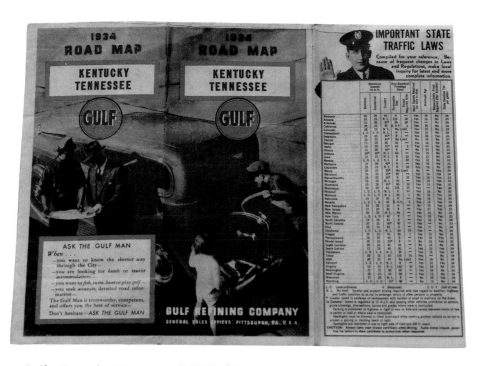

Gulf—New Orleans, $17-21

Gulf—Kentucky, Tennessee (1934), $20-26

Skelly—Wisconsin, $10-21

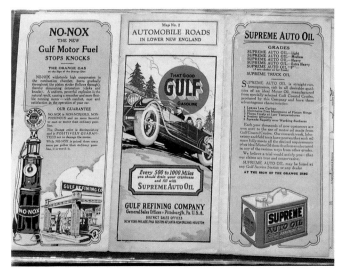

Gulf—Ontario Quebec, $25-31

Gulf—Lower New England, $25-31

Simms Oil Co.—Texas, $38-46

(reverse side of Simms Oil Co.)

Colonial, $37-43

Herring-Wissler Co.—Iowa, $20-26

D-X—Missouri, $35-41

D-X—Iowa, $30-36

Diamond 760—Iowa, $48-53

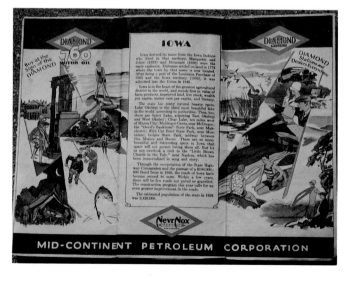

(reverse side of Diamond 760)

Cities Service—Missouri, $30-36

Colonial—1925, $48-53

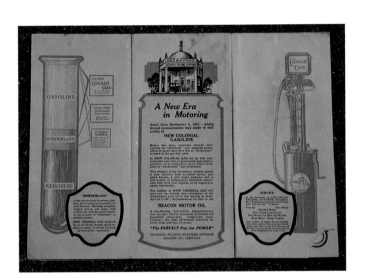

(reverse side of Colonial)

Champlin—Illinois, $17-21

Cities Service—New York, 1936, $20-25

Gulf—New York and Vicinity, 1939, $35-40

Socony-Vacuum—New York World's Fair, 1939, $35-45

Esso—New York and World's Fair, 1939, $35-45

Barnsdall—Nebraska, 1933, $55-65

(reverse side of map)

License Plate Attachments

This section is from the collection of Fred Hartson, who provided the photos and prices.

Flying A Giant Power, $90-160

Tydol man (yellow), $65-90

Pennzoil 'Safety,' $85-100

Amoco, $60-90

Ford, Let's Take It Easy, $80-95

Rice's Garage 'Safety First,' $60-70

Tydol man (white), $65-90

Silvertown Safety League, $55-65

Lion, Naturalube, $110-130

Fleet Wing, Safety Pays, $75-115

44

Standard Oil Research Car, $125-175

Mobil, Drive Safely, $85-125

Mobil, Flying Red Horse, $90-115

Sunoco (initials, LMS), $60-90

Veedol man, candy apple red, $65-90

Sunoco (initials, WMW), $45-70

Sunoco (U.S.A. First), $75-120

Marathon Running Man, $70-90

D-X, $75-120

Atlantic White Flash, $85-95

46

Pure, Safety First, $75-95

Shell with three flags, $60-80

Imperial Research Test Car, $85-140

Crown Central, Drive Safely, $70-100

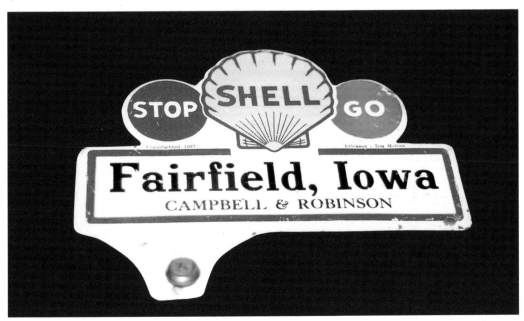

Shell, Stop Go, No Price Available

Cans

Panhandle Lubricants, five pound, $55-70

Hood Thread grease, one pound,
$75-140

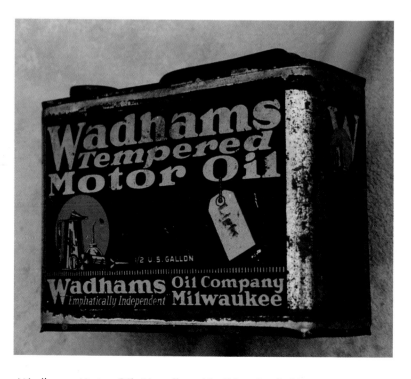

Wadhams Motor Oil, ½ gallon, No Price Available

Display of TROCO cans, No Price Available

Troco Oils ½ gallon (rare) No Price Available

'Red Head' Motor Oil, Imperial quart, $130-145

Primrose
'Speedoil' (small
can), $35-45

L. O. Church 'Zeroniz,' $95-115

Globe Lubricant,
one pound cup
grease, $45-55

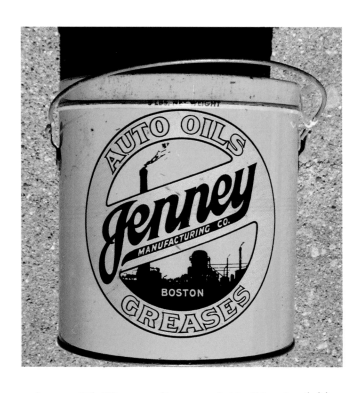

'Aroway' Motor Oils, two gallons, $65-75

Jenney Oils/Greases, five pound, No Price Available

Archer Lubricants, one pound cup grease, $30-40

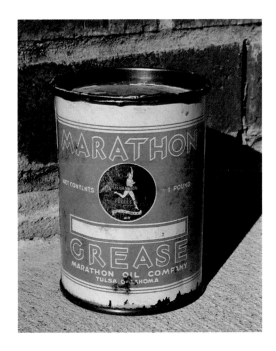

Marathon Grease, one pound cup grease, $45-55

Cosden Lubricant, one pound cup grease, $35-45

Golden Eagle Grease, one pound cup grease, $40-50

Barnsdall Grease, one pound cup grease, $15-25

Diamond Grease, one pound cup grease, $20-30

White Eagle Grease, one pound cup grease

(Shows eagle on side of White Eagle Grease) $40-50

Sunoco Lubricant, one pound cup grease, $40-50

Arctic Cup Grease (Standard Oil), one pound cup grease, $35-45

Cross Country Grease (Sears, Roebuck), one pound cup grease, $30-

Johnson Oils, one pound cup grease, $50-60

Cities Service Trojan Grease, one pound cup grease, $20-30

Marathon Lubricant, one pound cup grease, $35-45

Kendall Grease, one pound cup grease, $40-50

Capitol Lubricant, one pound, $25-35

Kenmore Aero Craft Motor Oil, $115-130

Phillips 44 Insect Killer, $95-115

Skydrol Hydraulic Fluid, one gallon, $10-16

DuPont Motor Oil Additive "7", $4-7

Autoplane Motor Oil, two gallon, No Price Available

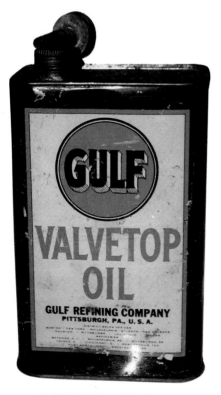

Gulf ValveTop Oil, $15-25

Mountain Oil Co., Inc., $150-175

Old Dutch, one pound cup grease, $275-375

Magnolia Grease, one pound cup grease, $150-225

Pep Boys 'Pure As Gold,' one pound cup grease, $65-90

Socony Vacuum 'Gargoyle,' one pound cup grease, $95-110

Quart Cans

Star Motor Oil cans, $80-100 each

(reverse side of Star cans)

Liquid Gold Motor Oil, $35-45

Gulf ColdFlo Antifreeze, $45-55

Archer Snowmobile & Outboard, $95-112

Cities Service Koolmotor Oil, $125-145

Sooner Queen Motor Oil, No Price Available

Tiger Motor Oil, $170-190

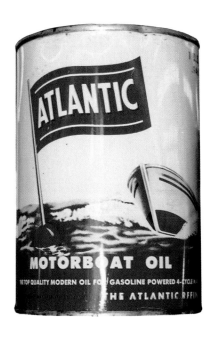

Atlantic Motorboat Oil, $160-200

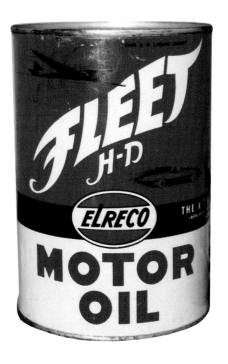

Fleet H-D 'Elreco' Motor Oil, $150-175

D-X Marine Oil, $225-360

(reverse side of D-X quart can)

Whippet Motor Oil, $230-270
Sooner State Oils, $350-395
Aero Mobiloil, $110-130

Pemco Motor Oil—Gasoline, $45-65

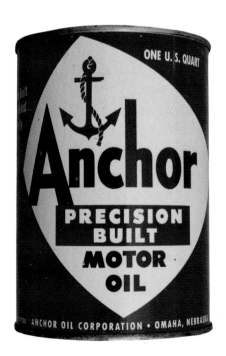

Anchor Motor Oil, $150-185

Eagle Motor Oil, $145-165

Ajax Motor Oil, $175-195
Wm. Tell Motor Oil, $135-155

Brahma Paraffin Base Oil, $300-360

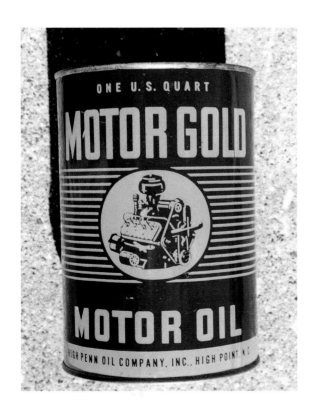

Motor Gold Motor Oil, $55-70

Avio Motor Oil, No Price Available

Fleet Wing Motor Oil, $75-95

Wings Motor Oil, $60-75

Texas City Motor Oil, $125-145

Oilzum Motor Oil, $220-255

Rislone Snowmobile Oil, $35-45

Kendall Motorcycle Oil, $50-70

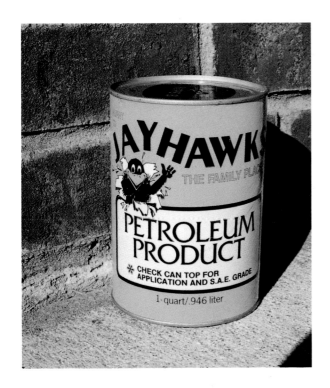

Jayhawk Petroleum Product, $20-35

Bardahl Racing Oil, $17-22

Elkolene Motor Oil, $115-130

Velvet Cushioned Motor Oil, $195-230

Golden Eagle Motor Oil, $160-180

Aero Mobiloil, green band, No Price Available
Aero Mobiloil, blue band, No Price Available

Sunfleet Engine Oil (composite material), $20-30

(reverse side of Sunfleet Engine Oil)

Golden West Motor Oil (composite material), $8-11

Cardinal Automatic Transmission Fluid, $18-22

Sunshine Motor Oil, $130-140

Royal Motor Oil, $35-45

Tesoro Petroleum Corp, $45-60 each

Fleet Motor Oil, $99-127

Sunset Motor Oil, No Price Available

HI-VAL-UE Motor Oil, No Price Available

Moly 'Black Gold' Motor Oil (composite material),
$30-40

Imperial 'Marvelube' Motor Oil (imperial quart), $40-50

Pumps

Gilbert Barco pump with Texaco etched globe, (pump) $850-1050, (globe) $675-875

Wayne Model 70 pump with Colonial globe, (pump) $850-1025, (globe) $350-550

Clock-Face pump with Royal 'Red Hat' globe, (pump)
$1125-122, (globe) $775-1200

Southwest pump with Liberty metal band globe, (pump)
$850-975, (globe) $1050-1250

Wayne Model 70 pump, $800-1000

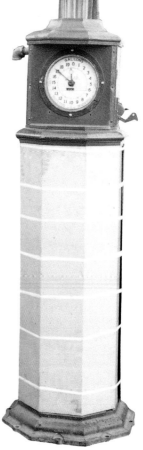

Mobilgas Special pump, $975-1150

Tokheim pump (not restored), $300-400

Gas pump, unknown maker (not restored), No Price Available

Tokheim pump (not restored) with D-X globe,
(pump), $300-400, (globe) $140-175

Wayne Model 60 clock-face pump, $1550-1800, with
reproduction Indian globe.

Early Wayne kerosene pump (model unknown), $550-675

(view of pump, open for operation)

(view of pump closed)

(close up)

Early Wayne curbside stroke pump, Model 864, $225-350

Tokheim 5-gallon model 290 (1923), $950-1200

Phillips curbside stroke pump, Model unknown, $175-250

Porcelain Gulf pump, $900-1250, with reproduction globe

Wayne clock-face pump with reproduction globe, Model 861B, $2000-2250. Gilmore tin sign, $475-550.

Kero Boy curbside stroke pump,
Model 555, $225-275

Curbside stroke pump, make and
model unknown, $175-250

Gulf National pump, Model A38,
$1650-1900

Red Crown Gasoline, 30", $200-350

Oak Motor Oil, 30", $600-1000

Mobilgas Ethyl, 30", $300-525

Marland Oils, 30", $250-500

Pratts Motor Oil, 30", $500-800

Loyal-Penn Motor Oil, 30", $500-800

Wadhams Gasoline, 30", $300-500

Shell-Penn Motor Oil, 30", $600-775

KanOtex Gasoline, 30", $450-600

Oilzum Motor Oils, 30", $750-1000

Flying A Service, 30" (beveled die-cut), $675-850

Sterling Gasoline, 30", $400-525

Phillips 66, 30", $400-600

Independent Gasoline/Motor Oil, 30", $250-375

Independent Gasoline, 30", $250-375

Skelly Aromax, 30", $450-575

Conoco Gasoline, 30", $400-600

'Be Square' Motor Oil, 30", $300-400

Cushing Gasoline, 30", $250-400

Eason Gasoline, 30", $300-400

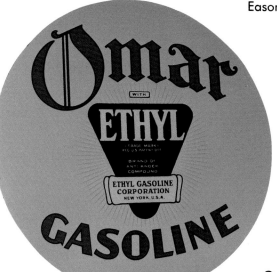

Omar Gasoline, 30", $350-500

White Eagle Gasoline (balanced), 30", $400-500

White Eagle Gasoline (banner), 30", $400-500

Polarine Motor Oil, 30", $225-300

Tydol Ethyl, 30", $400-500

Pennzip Gasoline, 30", $450-600

Purol Ethyl, 30", $375-500

Refiners Ethyl, 30", $400-525

Emblem Motor Oil, United Refining, 30", $375-475

Phillips Ethyl, 30", $700-900

Shellubrication, 30", $500-650

Violet Ray Gasoline (General), 30", $600-800

Red Hat Motor Oil and Gasoline, 30", $750-1000

Pioneer 'Dixcel' Gasoline, 36", $400-550

Caltex Lubricants (foreign), $36", $575-700

United Ethyl, 30", $500-650

Trop-Artic Motor Oils, 30", No Price Available

Manhattan Gasoline, 30", No Price Available

Pencoil, 30", $350-475

Shell Chassis & Motor Lubrication, 24", $400-550

M-F-A Gasoline, 42", $175-225

Refiners Gasoline & Motor Oils, 30",
$400-525

Chevron Credit Cards, 30", $225-325

Sunray Oils, 30", $600-750

Richardson's Motor Oil & Gasoline, 30", $225-300

Pan-Am 'Ethyl' Gasoline, 30", $325-425

Pennzoil Safe Lubrication, 24", $375-490

Iso-Vis Motor Oil (Standard Oil), 30", $400-525

Sunray Oils, 30", $275-350

Castrol Distributor, two-sided, 30", $350-400

'Brice Gasoline, two-sided, 30", $450-500

Crystal Gasoline, two-sided, $350-475

Miscellaneous

AMOCO Agricultural Chemical advertising sign, $175-225

'AC' Oil Filter, flanged, two-sided tin, $100-130

'Sparkie' flanged sign, $150-230

Aeroshell Lubricating Oil, No Price Available

AMOCO die-cut porcelain, $225-325

'American' credit card porcelain sign (medium size), $80-130

Bulko Gasoline, porcelain pump plate, No Price Available

Chevron, large porcelain sign, one-sided, $160-195

Cities Service rest room swing sign, two-sided, porcelain, $125-145

CONOCO (small, 24"), porcelain, $225-280

Continental Oil Company 'Coupons" accepted, one-sided tin, $118-140

Cooper Tires, one-sided painted tin, $38-60

Deep-Rock Motor Oil, porcelain, $375-525

Diamond 760 Motor Oil, porcelain, $150-230

Dodge Brothers sign, doubled-sided, porcelain, $250-300

DuPont Methanol Anti-Freeze card-board sign with painted tin frame, $50-125

EN-AR-CO Motor Oil, embossed tin, $300-450

ESSO, flanged porcelain (foreign), $325-450

Esso Elephant Kerosene porcelain sign, very unusual (foreign), No Price Available

Esso Aviation, painted tin sign (one-sided, rare), $525-640

'Flying A' porcelain sign, $70-100

Firestone tires, large one-sided porcelain, $130-160

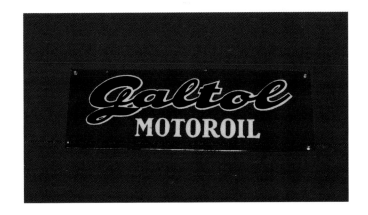

Galtol Motoroil, small porcelain sign, $90-118

Firezone painted sign, $70-80

Upper Cylinder Lubricant with Gargoyle porcelain cylinder sign (foreign), No Price Available

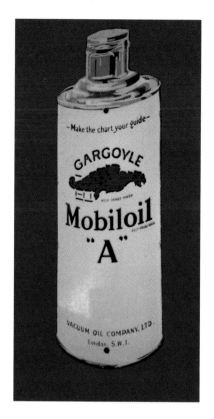

Gargoyle die-cut porcelain sign (foreign), $1800-2000

Gargoyle two-sided porcelain sign, $475-550

Gargoyle Mobiloil 'D' two-sided, porcelain (foreign), No Price Available

Gargoyle Mobiloil flanged two-sided porcelain sign (foreign), $325-400

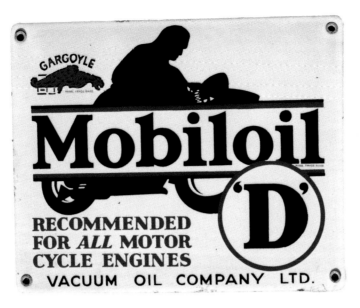

Gargoyle Mobiloil 'D,' motor cycle oil, porcelain, one-sided, $1450-1650

Gillette Tire/No Chains Needed, $175-250.

Die-cut cardboard sign, very nice, $175-250.

Goodrich Guide Post (one of the first highway markers prior to state-mandated highway signs), No Price Available

Goodrich Silvertown Tires porcelain sign, $475-550

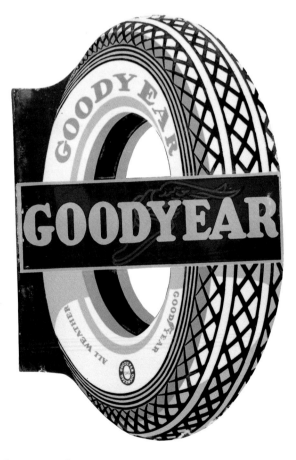

Goodyear Tire flanged two-sided die-cut porcelain sign, $550-625

Gulfpride Marine, porcelain, $325-500

Harris OILS—porcelain, $525-650

Humble porcelain rest room sign, $225-275

Humble Oil 'No Smoking,' porcelain one-sided, $80-110

Humble porcelain rest room sign, $225-275

Jayhawk Oils, painted tin, $325-450

Johnson Oils, flanged die-cut, painted tin,
$850-1000

Johnson die-cut cardboard radiator shield, $90-110

Framed Kelly sign, porcelain, $390-500

'Lion' gasoline porcelain sign (large, 5 foot, two-sided),
$250-325

MARS, one-sided embossed tin, $120-145

Michelin, porcelain, $200-500

Michelin Man for Michelin Tires die-cut porcelain sign, No Price Available

Michelin porcelain for air chart, No Price Available

Michelin Tire porcelain sign, $425-475

Michelin bicycle tires, small sign, $350-400.

Michelin, one-sided die-cut porcelain (foreign), $375-425

Mobil porcelain sign (hard to find), $150-300

Mobiloil Shield, Vacuum Oil Company, porcelain 16" x 16", $525-650

Mobilgas *Special* porcelain sign, $475-550

Mobiloil, large porcelain sign, $175-240

Mona Motor Oil, one-sided tin (notice radio station advertisement), $175-230

PENNO Motor Oil, painted tin, $125-160

Independent 'Gas and Oils' advertising piece (die-cut, painted tin), $195-285

Penn Motor Oil, painted tin, $120-160

Pennant Motor Oil, die-cut cardboard, $20-30

Pennant Kerosene flanged two-sided porcelain foreign sign
(notice Shell logo upper corner), $475-550

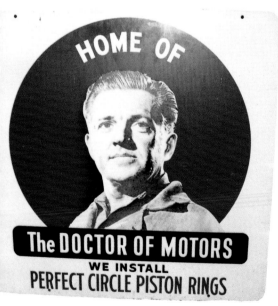

Perfect Circle Piston Rings advertising
piece, $160-185

Philgas Service (one-sided), porcelain, $365-450

Philgas Service (flanged two-sided), porcelain, $375-475

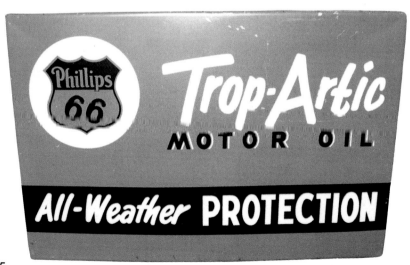

Phillips 'Trop-Arctic' tin oil-rack sign, $145-215

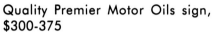

Quality Premier Motor Oils sign,
$300-375

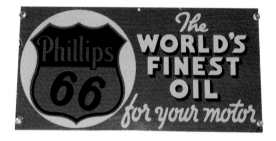

Porcelain signs: *Phillips 66 'World's
Finest Oil' (green sign), $475-525
Phillips 66 'World's Finest Oil' (red
sign), $475-525*

Pure Pep, Pure Oil Company, small,
round porcelain, $350-425

Quaker State painted tin, $95-135

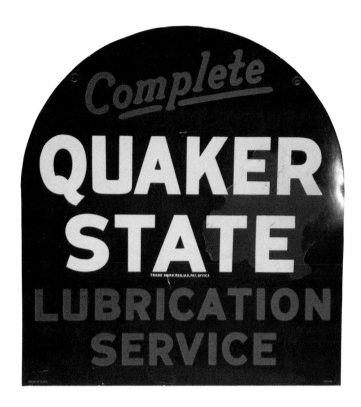

'Red Hat' Motor Oil, flanged, painted tin, $625-875

Quaker State swinging two-sided porcelain sign, $200-325

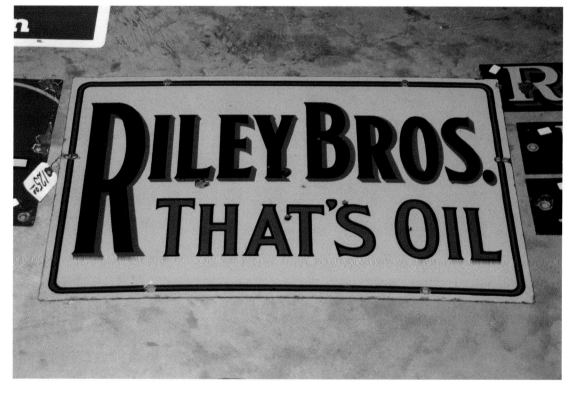

Riley Bros., porcelain, $95-140

Shell Motor Oil, small die-cut painted tin, No Price Available

SAXON Motor Cars (old), porcelain, No Price Available

"SHELL" Lubricating Oils early porcelain, two-sided sign, $180-290

Shell flanged die-cut porcelain sign
(foreign), $450-525

Shell porcelain triangle (foreign), $375-450

Shell *Specialised* Lubrication, large two-sided porcelain sign
(foreign), $350-450

Shell from the Pump, porcelain one-
sided (foreign), $550-600

113

Shell *from the* Pump early die-cut two-sided porcelain (foreign), $1500-1850

Shell Motor Spirit and Motor Oils flanged, porcelain (foreign), $450-600

Signal Oil and Gas Company door sign 6", porcelain, $250-325

Sinclair, small truck door sign, porcelain, $290-410

Sinclair porcelain sign, $250-395

All porcelain signs: Sinclair 'Opaline' motor oil (small sign on left), $400-575
Sinclair 'Opaline' motor oil (sign in middle), $850-1045
Sinclair 'Pennsylvania' motor oil (sign on right), $375-600

Sinclair Gasoline, die-cut cardboard, $90-125

Sinclair 'Gas Line' warning sign, small, porcelain, $125-230

Standard Oil Company "Safety First," porcelain, one-sided, $200-240

Sinclair Credit Card sign, two-sided (note credit card in upper right corner of sign), $85-110

Standard Oil 'Perfection Kerosene,' flanged, painted tin,
$160-185

Standard Oil Company, porcelain, one-sided, $200-240

Sunray D-X, (orange background)
small, porcelain, $490-650

Sunoco 'Car Saver,' porcelain, $150-225

Texaco cardboard sign, $45-60

Texas Garagements Assoc., porcelain
two-sided, $80-110

Sunray D-X, (white background) small,
porcelain, $390-480

Tiolene, Pure Oil Company, small,
round porcelain, $475-550

UNIFLO 'Happy Motoring' painted tin, $75-110

White Rose Gasoline & National Motor Oil, tin, $140-200

Universal Batteries, porcelain (very nice sign), $220-240

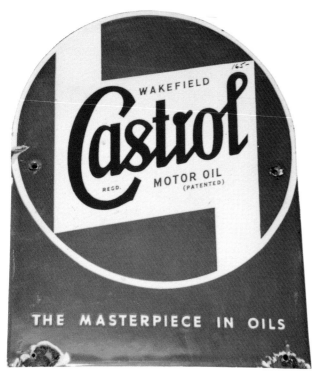

Castrol Motor Oil, small porcelain, $140-165

Wakefield *Castrol* Motor Oil flanged porcelain, $300-450

Wakefield CASTROL Motor Oil, one-sided porcelain sign
(foreign), $350-400

Wakefield CASTROL Motor Oil
flanged (foreign), $275-350

Oklahoma Ethyl porcelain pump plate, $200-300

Sunoco pump plate, porcelain, $125-180

Boyce-ite pump plate, brass, No Price Available

Ethyl pump plate, porcelain, $300-400

Ethyl 'Super 100' clock pump plate, porcelain, $125-325

Fina, small pump plate, porcelain, $200-300

Fina pump plate, porcelain, $200-300

'Flying A,' porcelain pump plate, $150-175

FRY porcelain pump plate $190-290

'GRIZZLY' gasoline porcelain pump plate, No Price Available

Gulf Marine White porcelain pump plate (newer), $100-130

Gulf pump plate, small, porcelain, $80-100

Knox porcelain pump plate, $290-385

MARS porcelain pump plate, $195-265

Metro pump plate, porcelain, $375-500

Mobil Avgas porcelain pump plate, $80-125

Mobilgas 'Special' pump plate, small, porcelain, $160-225

North Carolina Regular pump plate, porcelain, curved, $140-180

Richfield die-cut shield, two-sided, early, No Price Available

Royal, small, porcelain pump plate, $250-400

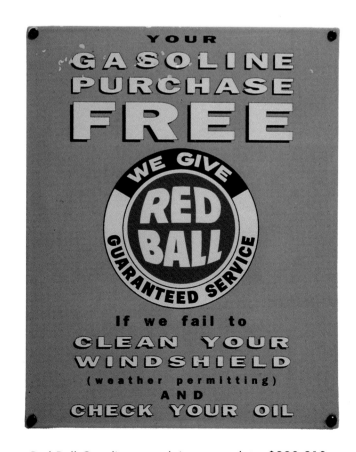

Red Ball Gasoline porcelain pump plate, $230-310

Top: Sinclair porcelain door sign, rare, $450-550
Bottom: Sinclair porcelain door sign, rare, $475-550

Standard White Crown porcelain pump plate, $75-95

TIME Super porcelain pump plate, $475-525

TIME Premium porcelain pump plate, $475-525

Cities Service Oils, lubster sign, porcelain, $175-260

VELTEX porcelain pump plate from Fletcher Oil Company, $190-300

'ESKO' Continental Oil Co. lubster sign, two-sided porcelain, (early, rare), No Price Available

Conoco lubster sign, early porcelain, $95-145

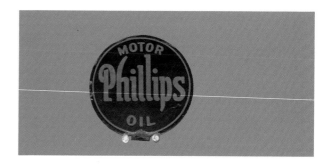

Phillips Motor Oil, lubster sign, porcelain, $375-525

Gargoyle Mobiloil lubster sign, porcelain, $165-295

Cities Service Oils, small porcelain curb sign, two-sided die-cut, $150-210

ATLAS curb sign, porcelain, $90-160

Polarine lubster sign, $225-250

Penn-Drake Motor Oil curb sign,
$545-625

Mother Penn Motor Oil curb sign (two-sided), porcelain,
$525-625

Phillips 66 Motor Oil, porcelain curb sign, 24", No Price
Available

Sinclair two-sided curb sign, early, $350-450

BATTERIES
SUPPLIES
GULF

Batteries-Supplies-Gulf, porcelain letters, $120-150

KanOtex, two-sided porcelain for neon (neon is missing),
$325-375

Shell, neon, die-cut sign, No Price
Available

Sohio and Skelly signs, neon, No Price Available

130

Phillips 66 and White Rose (neon signs), No Price Available

Shell porcelain sign and D-X, neon sign, No Price Available

Golden Tip Gasoline, Standard Oil, 76 (all neon), No Price Available

Vaught's 'Blue Blaze' Kerosene three-piece glass globe, $375-450

P.V.Q. 80 Ethyl three-piece glass globe, $450-500

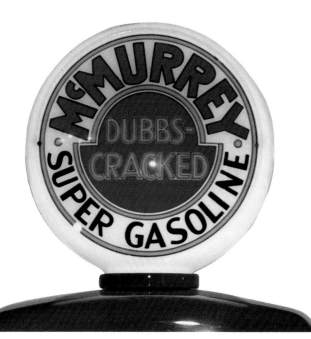

McMurrey Super Gasoline three-piece glass globe, $400-450

HiOtane "As New As Tomorrow" three-piece plastic body globe, $175-250

Oil Creek Refining gasoline globe, 15"
metal face, $300-375

Mobilgas 'Aircraft,' three-piece glass
globe, No Price Available

Golden Fleece plastic die-cut globe from Australia,
$130-165

Utility Gasoline on red ripple body,
$1200-1500

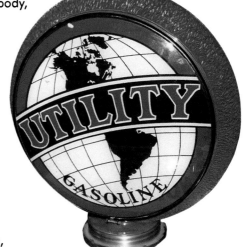

'ARO' Flight, three-piece plastic globe,
$200-250

Globe face for Gill body from Hill Oil Co. of Superior, Nebraska, $125-150

Penn Gas, one-piece etched gasoline globe, No Price Available

Mobiloil Gargoyle porcelain globe (foreign), very unusual, $475-650

United American Oil, globe with metal band, No Price Available

Gulf Kerosene, etched globe, $400-525

Richfield lenses for 15-inch globe, No Price Available

Socony globe with metal band, porcelain faces, $800-1025

General globe with metal band, $350-450

Farmers Union globe, ripple body, $475-600

Hoosier Pete globe, three-piece glass, $375-525

Mann's Gasoline globe, three-piece, $285-350

Sinclair gasoline globe with plastic attachment, $375-450

Anti-Knock gasoline globe, metal band, $275-325

Swanson Gasoline globe, metal band and face, $395-525

PUBLIX Gasoline globe, metal band, No Price Available

Gulf 'Marine White' globe, $350-650

PEMCO Regular Gasoline, plastic-body globe, $185-275
PEMCO Premium Gasoline, plastic-body globe, $185-275
Gulf 'ColdFlo' Antifreeze can, $45-55

Lexington Tires tire holder, $20-25

Fleet-Wing porcelain advertising piece, (very early), $125-200

Shell, cardboard advertising piece, No Price Available

Framed cardboard, No Price Available

Sunoco advertising piece, $250-300

Brownies 66 Service neon clock, No Price Availabie

Merry Christmas, neon clock, No Price Available

Burrs Service Station, neon clock, $575-650

Art Deco neon clock, $575-600

Cosden Petroleum and Mansfield Tire clock, $145-175

Quaker State Motor Oil Clock, $300-410

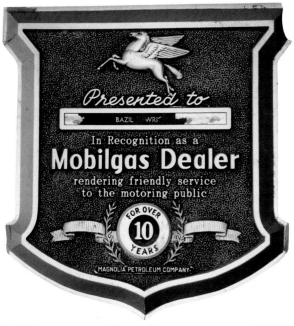

Mobil recognition plaque for over 10 years, $80-130

Socony-Vacuum Oil Co. recognition plaque, $115-135

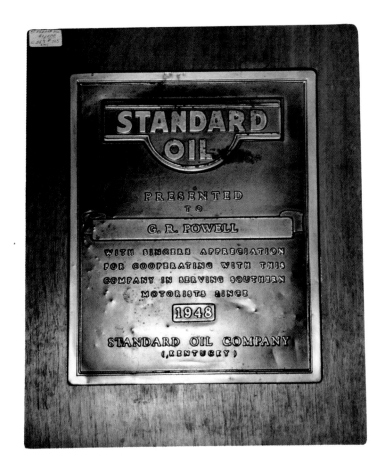

Standard Oil appreciation plaque, $30-60

Shell plaque, 5-year award, $45-75

'ECO' air pumps, No Price Available

'ECO' air tower, No Price Available

Air Meter, No Price Available

Mobiloil, concave one-sided sign with thermometer (Germany), $350-425

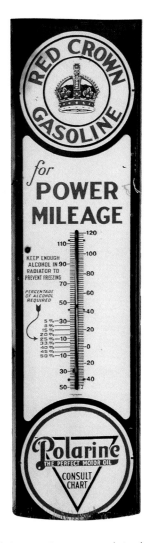

Small ashtray advertising gasket cement, $18-21

Red Crown, large porcelain thermometer, $675-800

Phillips 66 ash tray, $50-75

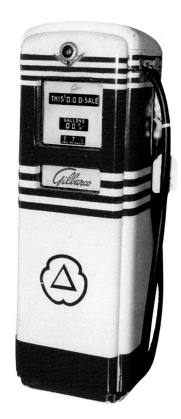

Cigarette Lighter/Dispenser, $600-775

'Gilmore Red Lion' match book, (front view of match book), $6-8

(back view of match book)

'Marathon' gasoline match book, $6-8

'Polly' gas match book, $6-8

Motor Age July 1944 magazine, Motor Age February 1944 magazine, $25-35 each

Motor Age February 1945 magazine,
Motor Age April 1945 magazine,
$25-35 each

Motor Age October 1945 magazine,
Motor Age June 1945 magazine,
$25-35 each

Interesting album cover for the Texaco collector, No Price
Available

'Filling Station Employee' pin-back,
$25-40

'Use Texhoma Products' pin-back,
$28-35

'Merry Christmas Esso,' 1940 pin-
back, $35-45

Mobil AV1 pin back, new, $22-38

AeroShell pin back, 1993, $22-38

Shell badge (seniority #17) from
Roxanna Refinery, No Price Available

Gulf Attendants Badge, $175-300

Conoco, product advertising pin-
back, $60-90

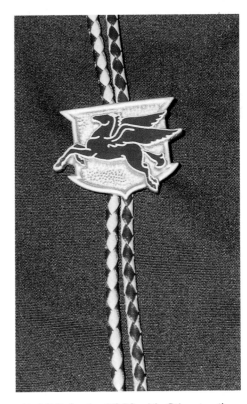

Mobil Bolo-tie, 1950s, No Price Available

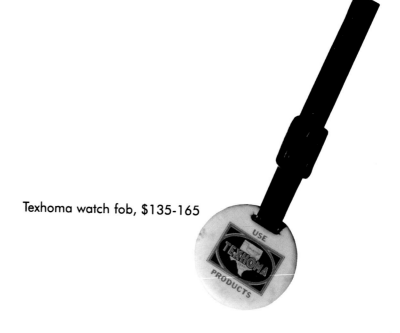

Texhoma watch fob, $135-165

'Magnolia Gasoline watch fob, No
Price Available

Chevron (unleaded) ID tag, two-sided porcelain, $10-16

Chevron ID tag, two-sided porcelain, $10-16

Gulf, round plastic rest room key holders, $50-70

Indian Refining, small decal, $4-6

Invincible Oil "R" pocket mirror, $85-110

ServiShine Glass and Metal Cleaner, tin by Phillips 66, $100-200

Mobil Penetrating Oil, Mobil Upperlube, Mobil Hand Lotion, $25-35 each

Mobil Lustre Cloth, Andy Glaze Auto Paint Preserver, Pit-Bar Magna Kloth dust cloth, $45-52 each

Mobiloil bottles, $60-70 each

Aero Mobiloil jar, 1940s, $125-155

Texaco Car Cleaner and Wax, Whiz *one stop* Polish, Liberty Polish metal cleaner, Liquid Glass auto polish, $35-45 each

Standard White Oil #9, Standard Hand Separator Oil, $40-50 each

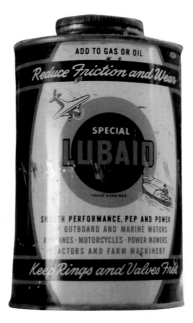

Lubaid gas or oil additive, $40-60

Chevron Starting Fluid, $45-55

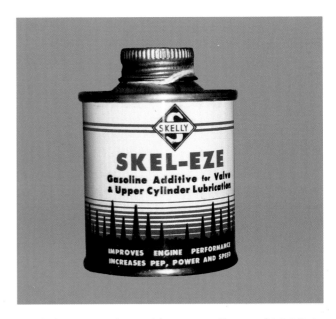

Skel-Eze Gasoline additive, (small can), $18-28

151

Sunoco Outboard Motor Oil, tin, $7-10

Fina, small tin, $15-30

Bardahl, small tin, $15-30

Bardahl 'Fuel System Treatment' (tin), $4-8

DeMert 'HEET' anti-freeze (tin), $4-8

Union Penetrating Oil, $70-85

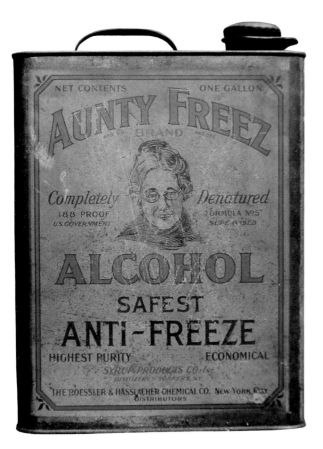

'Aunty Freez' Alcohol Anti-Freeze, $150-200

Phillips brass fire extinguisher, $140-170

(embossed on top of extinguisher)

Conoco dinner plate, $65-75
The dinnerware is from the collection of Tom Davidson, who provided the plates and prices.

AMOCO desk lamp, $65-90

154

Sun Oil Company dinner plate, $70-85

Sunoco cup, $65-75

Billups cup and saucer, $70-85

Union 76 bread plate, $35-45

Standard Oil Company, Indiana, chili bowl, $90-120

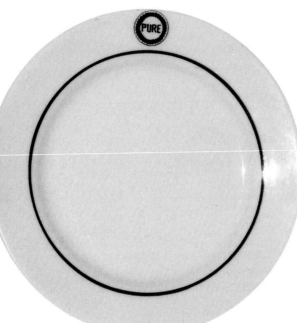

Standard Oil Company serving bowl, $175-225

Pure Oil Company bread plate, $35-50

ESSO dinner plate, $85-110

Mobil dinner plate, $70-80

Enco first aid kit, $75-95

Dominion Engine Oil plate by Standard Oil Co. (promotional item sold at Standard stations), $60-90

'Naptha Launches' plate by Standard Oil Co. (promotional item sold at Standard stations), $60-90

Flying Red Horse Radiator Mascot (rare), $400-575

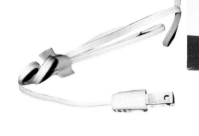

Kendall Oil, paper cap for advertising, $30-40

Time Oil Company alarm clock, No Price Available

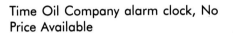

Stock certificate and credit card from Blue Bird Oil Company (rare), No Price Available

Standard of California children's game, Mickey Mouse and Donald Duck "Race to Treasure Island," $160-180

Shell display, No Price Available

Shell display, No Price Available

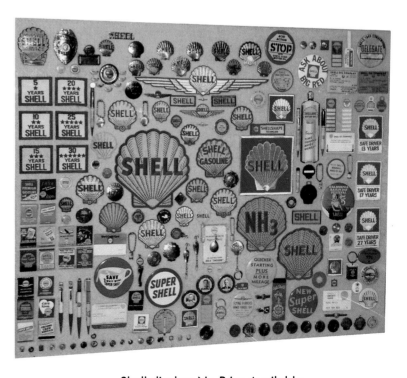

Shell display, No Price Available

Shell display, very nice, No Price Available

Sinclair display, No Price Available

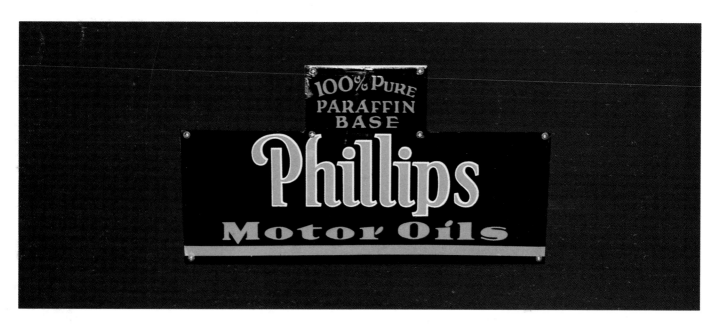

Phillips Motor Oils—front of oil-rack stand, porcelain, extremely rare, $525-675